SOFT TARGETS

How Donald Trump's Refusal to Place His Assets
into a Blind Trust is Inviting Terrorism and
Endangering the Lives of Thousands of Americans

By K.D. Bellston

I0406855

Rampart Communications Company
PO Box 2568
Toledo OH 43606

ISBN-13: 978-1543105407

ISBN-10: 1543105408

Dedication

This book is dedicated to my wife, mother, and family, all of whom have helped shape me into being a better person...

K.D. Bellston

Table of Contents

01 INTRODUCTION. 7

02 ENTER DONALD TRUMP --THE MOST HATED MAN IN THE WORLD. (AND, SADLY, HE LIKES IT.) 13

03 WHAT IS A BLIND TRUST (AND WHY DO POLITICIANS USE THEM?) 19

04 SOFT TARGETS – EACH AND EVERY TRUMP TENNANT 25

05 FIRST, WHAT IS A "HARD TARGET"? 29

06 STRETCHING THE SECRET SERVICE THIN 33

07 THE TRUMP TARGETS! 37

08 TRUMP TOWER – TRUMP'S CROWN JEWEL AND PRIME TARGET 39

09 THE TRUMP SOFT TARGETS! 43

10 ONE GOOGLE SEARCH AWAY 53

11 TRUMP'S NAME INVITES TERRORISM 85

12 HOW TERRORISTS CHOOSE THEIR TARGETS 89

13 TRUMP'S OBLIGATION TO RELEASE TENANTS FROM THEIR LEASES................95

14 A CALL FOR LEGISLATION... OR CONSTITUTIONAL AMENDMENT... OR... AT LEAST THE COURTS... 99

ENDNOTES...102

ABOUT THE AUTHOR 106

"There were people that were cheering on the other side of New Jersey, where you have large Arab populations. They were cheering as the World Trade Center came down."

Donald J. Trump, Nov 21, 2015

01 Introduction.

I sincerely hope that none of what I write about in this book ever comes to pass. I sincerely hope that the people who lease space from Donald Trump, or visit the individuals and businesses that lease space from Donald Trump, are never the targets of a terrorist attack. I genuinely wish that terrorism ceased to exist, and that the political process would evolve to the point where everyone feels that they are at least getting their political voices heard and given some weight.

But what I want does not really influence the world very much. Instead what I see as a likely outcome of the Trump Presidency is an increase in hate between ethnic groups, and countries. I see it being very likely that the protests Donald Trump has already inspired because of his own virulent rhetoric, and his mass of white supremacist followers, are going to continue to grow.

As a result of this, I foresee that Donald Trump, by grabbing as much glory as he can, and trying to turn America into a Trump Autocracy, is going to inspire a lot of terrorism. Maybe a war also, or a few, but we will cross that bridge, or bridges when it is time. For now my desire is to simply discuss the obviousness of Trump properties, and the people associated with them, as being obvious targets for terrorism.

Perhaps I am being paranoid. Perhaps you, good reader, will pour over my words and decide that I am being incredibly simplistic, naïve, delusional, or otherwise wrong. Perhaps you feel that Donald Trump has inspired a new wave of terrorism, where the people who shoot, bomb, poison, immolate, drown, and otherwise kill innocent people, would never be so rude as to attack one of the hundreds of Donald Trump properties in an attempt to grab glory and "make it personal".

In all candor, if you feel that way, I think you are being delusional. I do respect your right to feel that way, and express disdain for my views.

But I think you are wrong.

I am not going to go into detail on all the possibilities for all the terror attacks that could be played out on Donald Trump properties and events. I am also not going to highlight just how vulnerable each and every Trump endeavor is. But what I will do instead is to pick a few properties at random and demonstrate how easy it would be to take a previously successful terror attack, dust it off, and apply it to the Trump property.

Having said that, there will be critics who claim that this book might inspire people to engage in terror attacks, or that I am somehow risking planting ideas in the minds of people who are otherwise prone to violence. To those people I would ask, "What book was the inspiration for 9/11?"

"What book inspired the 1927 Bath School Bombing?"

"What book inspired the 1838 Mormon War that led to the state of Missouri legalizing the murder of Mormons?"

"What book inspired the September 16, 1920 Wall Street Bombing?"

America has never lacked for terrorist attacks. During our 240 years as a nation we have seen hundreds of major terrorist attacks, and thousands of minor ones. The vast majority of these were inspired by nothing but hate.

Also note a very important fact: it is insane to think that terrorists are not already targeting Donald Trump properties. If I came up with such an idea so quickly into the Trump Presidency, would not it be insane to think that I was the first person to think of it? Would not it also be insane to think that I would have been the only person to think of it? Who in their right mind would think that had I not published this book, out of the billions of human beings on Planet Earth who would be actively thinking for roughly 16 hours a day, 365 days a year, for at least four years, I would be the only one to have ever thought of this?

I have news for the people who would criticize this book as something that should not have been written – the terrorist are already planning these activities. They are already discussing and planning the targeting of Trump properties. What that means is that somebody needs to alert everyone who is a visitor to any Trump property, or works in any Trump property, or lives in any Trump property, that they could become the next major terrorist statistic.

Human beings have a right to be made aware of the fact that they are far more likely to be the subject of a terror attack visiting a Trump facility than if they are instead visiting a local shopping mall. Law enforcement needs to be made aware of the fact that they need to spend additional resources protecting the people that are in Trump properties. Citizens need to be made aware of the fact that Trump properties are inherently more likely to be targets of terror attacks while Donald Trump is President, so that they can simultaneously demand additional steps be taken to protect people from terror attacks on those properties, while avoiding those properties themselves.

I also face a dilemma of whether or not to publish a list of Trump owned properties. Some people would argue that I am alerting potential terrorists of targets when I point out that the Central Park Carousel, or Miss Teen USA Pageants are owned by Donald Trump. My response to those critics is very straightforward – none of the targets that I list are properties that are not widely known to be Donald Trump properties. As part of my methodology in demonstrating how publicly available a list of Trump properties are, I am going to be describing a very rudimentary Google search using just the search terms "Donald Trump assets " and the laundry list of Trump properties said search will turn up.

The terrorists know how to use Google. I give them that much credit. You should as well.

So I have decided to list many of the properties which such a rudimentary search revealed. I know of no other way to cause public debate over this issue, so that people are informed of the vulnerability of these properties, and the vulnerability of the people within those properties, unless I actually show just how public that list of properties is.

Of course, this book would become 100% moot if Donald Trump simply followed through on his promise to place his assets into a blind trust. But the only thing that can be said about Donald Trump with any degree of certainty is that he does not care about the people he is supposed to be serving, but instead loves his money.

I hope that Donald Trump begins to love his fellow human beings more than he loves his money, and places his properties into a blind trust, so as to eliminate these obvious soft targets from inviting terrorism. I do not think that is likely to happen, because there is no way Donald Trump is not already keenly aware of the fact that his properties are an open invitation to terrorism – but as long as he can keep making money off of them, that is what he is going to do. Thus, it is my secondary hope that he will release tenants from their leases, so that people can decide to not be part of the human shields protecting Donald Trump's fat checking account.

Barring that I hope Donald Trump is held accountable in the Courts, as any other landlord would be for inviting terrorism onto the people he leases to.

Sincerely,

K.D. Bellston

"Donald J. Trump is calling for a complete and total shutdown of Muslims entering the United States until our country's representatives can figure out what the hell is going on."

Donald J. Trump, Dec 7, 2015.

02 Enter Donald Trump --The Most Hated Man in the World. (And, Sadly, He Likes It.)

The last time the election of an American president divided the country this much, and led to such massive protests, it was Abraham Lincoln who had won, and America went rushing directly into a Civil War.

Already Donald Trump's views and policies, all aimed against people with skin not as white as his own, are causing people in countries around the globe to openly express revulsion and contempt at Donald Trump. Former steadfast allies around the globe are publicly expressing outrage over the idiotic tyrant which has been handed a large amount of control of the power of the United States of America.

And how has Donald Trump reacted to this massive outpouring of open and bitter hatred expressed at him?

Why, he has spent much of his political capital delivering Tweets directed at those who oppose him, and attacking Nordstrom for refusing to continue to carry the failing "Ivanka" line of overpriced inferior goods that simply were not selling.

We have a President whose inability to comprehend what the duties of being a President are, is only surpassed by his joyous glee in his ability to inspire millions of people to feel hate towards him.

Donald Trump revels in being feared by his staff. He revels in being loved by people who think he will do good things for them. But he also revels in being hated by anyone who does not love him. Being despised is Donald Trump's dysfunctional way of at least getting some reaction out of people who will not love him, nor fear him. Like a self-destructive teenager crying out for attention because they feel unloved and alone, Donald Trump takes active steps to cultivate people into hating him. He expresses scorn and contempt for anyone whose views differ from his own. He makes outrageous juvenile insults towards anyone who publicly disagrees with him.

Donald Trump and his followers claim that this is merely Donald Trump avoiding "political correctness", and demonstrates that he is a "straight shooter" who always "speaks his mind".

While it is true that Donald Trump says whatever kind of half-baked thoughts that immediately leap into his brain, it must be noted that Donald Trump takes great pride in being intentionally abusive towards others. He takes a great pride in using derisive racial slurs towards anyone not of Northern European descent who contradicts him, or stands in his way. Any woman who does not smile and giggle when he "walks up and grabs their pussy" – or the verbal equivalent of that activity – is immediately derided on their weight, looks, or menstrual cycle timing. Despite the fact that Donald Trump has bragged about the fact that he has never asked for forgiveness under the doctrines of the Christian theology, Donald Trump does not even hide the fact that he believes most or all Muslims are terrorists who should be kept out of America, and probably nuked.

Donald Trump inspires hate for himself, and America, in volumes that no other President has ever been able to achieve.

In just a few short weeks of office, he has attempted to take absolute control of the United States government. Through a flurry of executive actions unseen since the beginning of World War II, Donald Trump has attempted to remold America into the intolerant and bigoted country that his followers crave. As he has met with resistance, and our rightful stoppage of his dreams, his childish antics, and Tweets, have simply grown more and more tyrannical.

Instead of wielding power he thought was going to be absolute, he has encountered a series of governmental checks and balances, and an ever vigilant press and populace. The more Donald Trump attempts to do in achieving his autocratic worldview, the more resistance he encounters.

And the more resistance he encounters, the more he is pressing back against it. Anyone who highlights his failings, corruption, or the corruption of his staff, is viciously attacked by Donald Trump. He has already taken steps to begin spying on all of the Civil Servants that are working under him. He has publicly attacked America's spy agencies as criminals for their part in publicly exposing the criminal activities of his staff members.

Eventually, that means that there will be violence inspired by this man, and the amount of terror attacks we would otherwise endure is going to escalate. The more that Trump feels powerless because his dictatorial desires are checked and balanced by the Constitution and other branches of government, the more he is going to act out like any other spoiled brat or petty tyrant. Logically, it follows that the more that Trump acts out like a spoiled child – the more that he tries to force America, and the world, to bend to his will – the less people are going to put up with it. And the less that people are willing to put up with it, the higher the number of people that will be willing to turn to violence against Donald Trump and, sadly, America.

It is unfortunate that some people will feel this way. The more that Donald Trump grows frustrated and verbally lashes out at anyone or anything that reins him in, the more proof there is that our Democratic process works. The reality of the Trump administration is that so far it has been incredibly ineffective at actual change – at least compared to what he wanted and said that he would achieve – with his grandiose plans being quickly reined in by the courts, Congress, and press.

But not all people are rational. The more that Donald Trump tries to force America and the world to bend to his will, the more some people are just not going to like it. There are irrational people out there who will, over time, begin to hate Donald Trump more and more. Some of these people will be members the far left who feel he is going too far. Some will be members of the right who feel that he is not going far enough and has sold them out. Some will simply be insane, and will pick Donald Trump as a target for their focus of anger because in their psychotic state it makes sense to them.

In the past, directing violence towards the president has been very difficult. Terrorists have had to accept venting their anger on such things as public events, or federal buildings. Periodically some of them might attack a shopping mall, nightclub, or mass transit system. Usually the target of the terrorist act has been some convenient soft target venue, with the hardened government targets being the exclusive domain of the professional terrorists. An example of the former would be the Boston Marathon Bombing which attacked a public footrace and beer-fest, while an example of the latter would be the massive devastation of 9/11.

In the era of Donald Trump, it is a little bit different. Any terrorist that wants to attack Donald Trump directly has the previously unavailable opportunity to attack the President of the United States by simply blowing up his buildings, personal aircraft, and the added targets of being able to kill his tenants. They can also attack Donald Trump's events, simultaneously hurting a man they hate, while also earning the recognition of having harmed President Trump directly.

The sad reality is that Donald Trump is creating a situation that invites terror attacks on his property. He loves to put the Trump name on everything. He loves to brag about how rich he is. Choosing to attack his property is no more inventive than keying somebody's paint job on their car. Attacking someone's pride and joy, or something they love, is as common as slicing someone's tires. To think that attacking Trump properties is something that terrorists have not already thought of requires one to be intentionally ignorant of the fact that for tens of thousands of years, hundreds of millions of people who have held nothing more than petty grudges have attacked the homes, vehicles, horses, crops, tools, children, clothes, food, and drink of the people that they hated. One would have to be incredibly ignorant of the human reality to not know that these "paybacks" are usually incredibly out of proportion to the perceived wrong that the aggrieved party feels.

Thus, no matter how irrational it is to attack a Trump property in retaliation for whatever wrong some people feel that he has done to them, or humanity in general, unless human nature changes overnight, tomorrow is going to see either terror attacks on Trump properties, or planning of terror attacks on Trump properties.

That is not speculation; it is – looking at human nature – a certainty.

"When Mexico sends its people, they're not sending the best. They're sending people that have lots of problems and they're bringing those problems. They're bringing drugs, they're bringing crime. They're rapists and some, I assume, are good people, but I speak to border guards and they're telling us what we're getting."

Donald J. Trump, June 16, 2015

03 What is a Blind Trust (and Why Do Politicians Use them?)

Donald Trump could stop this open invitation to attack his properties by placing them in a blind trust. Once that step was taken, no one would know – for sure – whether or not Donald Trump still owned the properties in question. Maybe he would, maybe he wouldn't. Such uncertainty would remove these open and easy targets from being a "guaranteed hit" on Donald Trump by terrorists

Back when he was running for office, Donald Trump promised that he would place all of his assets into a blind trust and walk away from controlling his considerable assets and companies. This campaign promise was made to assure people that there would be no conflict of interest if Donald Trump were to actually win the presidency and be sworn in as President of the United States. The theory behind a politician placing his or her assets into a blind trust is that this will theoretically prevent said politician from being able to engage in "self-dealing". A public official would have the ability, at least theoretically, to sometimes influence their governmental department into making better deals involving the property or company owned by said politician.

An example of self-dealing would be a mayor of a city, which we will just happen to call ... Los Angeles, who owns a condominium that the city of Los Angeles is considering purchasing for expansion of some civic function. For example, they might want the land which the mayor owns in order to build a new bus terminal, or offer to a large company, at a discount rate, as an incentive for said company to locate a manufacturing facility on that site. It does not take much imagination to see that the mayor of Los Angeles would be able to exert incredible pressure on the staff that works underneath him or her to come up with a "fair" offer for the City to offer as a purchase price for the property.

Naturally, the mayor would consider the actual dollar amount of what would be "fair" to be considerably higher than what city planners, commissioners, or taxpayers would consider "fair".

Now, it would be ludicrous for there to be ethics requirements that state any and all government employees are prohibited from owning property on the off chance that someday the government might want to deal with, purchase, lease, or otherwise become financially involved with said properties. The odds of such an event taking place are rather low, and temporary protections can be installed to prevent self-dealing should a situation like that arise.

When it comes to the President of the United States however, each and every decision which they make can have dramatic effects on each and every business in the United States of America. A president that owns a large number of shares of several Fortune 500 companies in the technology sector will have a keen interest in advancing laws and regulations that advance the technology sector of commerce. Conversely, should there be a proposal for a tax increase, or additional regulations on America's technology sector, that president would have a very keen interest to oppose any and all such regulations.

Laws or policies that would help the technology sector would be far more likely to be passed and signed by the president into law. Laws and policies which would hinder the technology sector would likely be opposed and vetoed. This natural tendency towards self-enrichment invites politicians to advance their personal interests over the interests of the population at large.

Presidents, and presidential candidates, universally put their assets into blind trusts as a way of assuring the American voters that they will perform their duties in an unbiased way that advances America's overall best interest. It is a way of making sure that the President, when they take office, rule a little bit more with their head, and a little less thinking about their own checkbook.

The details of a blind trust are fairly straightforward – the assets are placed into a blind trust for the benefit of the person making the trust, also known as the beneficiary. A person or team of people is named the trustee. It is the trustee's job to administer the assets of the trust in a way that protects the assets, and if possible, increases their value. The assets can also be sold or liquidated as needed. For example, if one of the companies in the trust portfolio is performing poorly, the trustee can sell it off, take the proceeds, and invest in something more profitable. Should there be an investment opportunity presented to the trustee that appears worthwhile, the trustee may invest in said endeavor.

The trustee is given a task to act in a way that increases the trust's value, while simultaneously protecting it from loss.

Normally in a blind trust situation, once the possible conflict of interest has been resolved – such as the Mayor leaves office – the blind trust can be dissolved, and the original party, or designated replacement, is assigned to take control of the assets.

Because of his considerable assets, Bill Clinton placed his properties into a blind trust when he became president. George W. Bush, also with a considerable portfolio, placed his investments into a blind trust so as to avoid any appearance of conflict of interest. Hillary Clinton, in 2007 when she began to run for President, placed her assets in a blind trust, where they remain to this day. Even rich ultra-millionaire Mitt Romney made a vow that he would place his assets into a blind trust if he was elected president in 2012.

Our Congress is full of Representatives, and Senators, who currently have assets in a blind trust. Many state lawmakers also place their assets in a blind trust. Indeed, the practice is so common that US law recognizes a blind trust made for this kind of purpose, and calls it a "Qualified Blind Trust", or QBT. These blind trusts have their own set of laws, regulations, case law, and tax rules. There are companies and law firms that specialize in handling these kinds of trusts.

Blind trusts are common for rich politicians to use.

Yet, despite the fact that Donald Trump swore that he would place his assets into a blind trust, he has not, and refuses to. This a promise which like so many other of his promises he has already broken or abandoned a mere few weeks into his administration.

But, this book is not about Donald Trump's lies to the public, his greed, his cavalier disregard for even the most basic attempts to avoid the appearance of impropriety, or the fact that within four weeks of taking office the list of his conflicts of interest grows and grows and grows. This is not the concern of this book.

If Donald Trump wants to use the office of the presidency to siphon money from the taxpayers to his own offshore bank accounts via executive actions that enrich him further, that is up to his conscience. If the American people do not care enough about his self-dealing to rise up and demand that Congress remove him from office, that is up to them. Instead what I am here to discuss is the fact that Donald Trump's refusal to put his assets into a blind trust is giving terrorists a very public list on exactly which businesses and properties to target for mass destruction and instant infamy.

"I will build a great wall -- and nobody builds walls better than me, believe me --and I'll build them very inexpensively. I will build a great, great wall on our southern border, and I will make Mexico pay for that wall. Mark my words."

Donald J. Trump, June 16, 2015

04 Soft Targets – Each and Every Trump Tennant

Donald Trump's refusal to place his assets into a blind trust is placing the lives of thousands of United States citizens, and the lives of international citizens, at risk. His willful disregard of even the most basic requirements that a President have no conflicts of interest during their presidency is not merely vilely repugnant, it is also dangerous.

Every day, people who work in a Donald Trump owned property, work in a business which is leasing from a Donald Trump company, lives in a residence owned by Donald Trump, or visits any of those people and places, are unknowingly walking into the crosshairs of some of the easiest, softest, and most inviting terrorist targets which any person could ever foolishly stumble into.

Let me be abundantly clear, and state it again: I think it is repugnant that Donald Trump is refusing to place his business assets into a blind trust, but if the American people are willing to let this slick huckster use the Office of the Presidency to advance his own financial gain, and the financial gain of his immediate family, that is on the American people. If they want their president to openly flout ethical considerations that even Manuel Noriega or Baby Doc Duvalier would have been ashamed to openly violate, who am I to argue? Bring on the bread and circuses as the rest of the world laughs as Americans publicly roll around in their own filth chanting "Donald, Make Us Great Again—Make Us Great Again!"

Simply put, not my concern. In truth, I consider America placing Donald Trump in the position of President as being a mistake which, sadly, America wanted to make at this point in time. We will pay a hefty price for having done it, will learn from our mistake, and at the end of four years be embarrassed that we could have failed so miserably.

But, that is for another day.

What is my current concern, however, is the fact that every last one of Donald Trump's properties is a soft target – a target which even the most backwards hayseed-chewing Christian fundamentalist, or Muslim extremist, could attack with less planning that it takes to rob a pizza delivery driver. Donald Trump owns at least 515 businesses and/or properties that he has admitted to owning. Furthermore, he likes to slap his name on as many of these as is practical – that being practical from the mindset of a man with a gold toilet who likes to openly associate with white supremacists.

What that means is there are actually hundreds of businesses and properties that bear the Trump name, making a very long "short list" of properties to attack.

Don't believe me?

Trump Tower, Trump University, Trump Steaks, Trump International Golf Course West Palm Beach, Trump Tower Manila, Trump National Golf Club Westchester, Trump International Hotel and Tower (Chicago); Trump Model Management, Trump AC Casino Marks LLC, and so on, and so on, and so on…. At this point it is tempting to rattle off 50 or 60 "Trump" properties or companies to illustrate just how many targets Donald Trump owns that openly advertise, "Terrorists! Deliver your suicide and car bombs here!", but that would only be scratching the surface. Donald Trump in 2015 supplied the Federal Election Commission with a list of all entities in which he serves as an executive. Out of the 515 listed in the disclosure, 268 of them contained the egotistical and terror-inviting "Trump" name.

"I think Islam hates us. There's a tremendous hatred. We have to get to the bottom of it. There is an unbelievable hatred of us."

Donald J. Trump, March 9, 2016

05 First, what is a "Hard Target"?

The White House is a hard target – terrorists would have to work very hard to do any kind of major damage to it. The last time there was a credible attack aimed at the White House which had a chance of causing the Secret Service, Department of Defense, or Department of Homeland Security any real difficulties was Flight 93 on September 11, 2001. Passengers overwhelmed the hijackers of that "Fourth Plane", and prevented it from reaching the White House[1].

Since that time, the ground, underground, and air security protecting the White House precludes any attack short of a Russian ICBM from having a snowball's chance of success. The periodic toy store drone might make it over the fence, or some whack-job nut might hop the fence and make it a few dozen feet towards the building before being gang-tackled by Secret Service. But aside from that, getting anywhere near harming the President while in the White House is, well... more people win the Super Lotto every year than make it ten feet beyond that fence uninvited.

Terrorists will not be able to get to Donald Trump in the White House unless they come up with some very well-financed "Mission Impossible" style plan.

While out on the road, or vacationing the President is probably pretty safe as well. Aside from a comical shoe-throwing incident which took place in Iraq on December 14, 2008, the last time a would be attacker got near a President was on March 30, 1981, when John Hinckley managed to shoot then President Ronald Reagan. The last successful assassination attempt on a US President was of course the assassination of John F. Kennedy by Lee Harvey Oswald on November 22, 1963. Thus, depending on how you look at it, the Secret Service has done an incredibly good job of protecting presidents and their close families, and of course presidential candidates, for either 36 years or 53 years. Based upon how mobile the presidents of the United States are, and how public their appearances are, this track record shows an incredibly high degree of competency, professionalism, and success by the Secret Service.

Figure 1. President Ronald Reagan March 30, 1981. The President waves to people outside the Washington Hilton Hotel seconds before John Hinckley, Jr. shoots him and also White House Press Secretary James Brady, who was left partially paralyzed and, decades later, died from complications of the wounds he received.

An examination of the assassination attempt on President Reagan shows how the Secret Services is very well trained, and skilled, at looking like they are not the elite task force which they are. The above photo shows "The Gipper" giving obligatory waves to people as he is escorted in a public venue. Milling around him appear to be staff minions who look like they are thinking of other things and are... well... almost bored. This scene looks more like someone running for Governor and losing than the entourage and President of the World's most powerful nation.

But, as Figure 2 will show, this scene is not as unguarded as it seems.

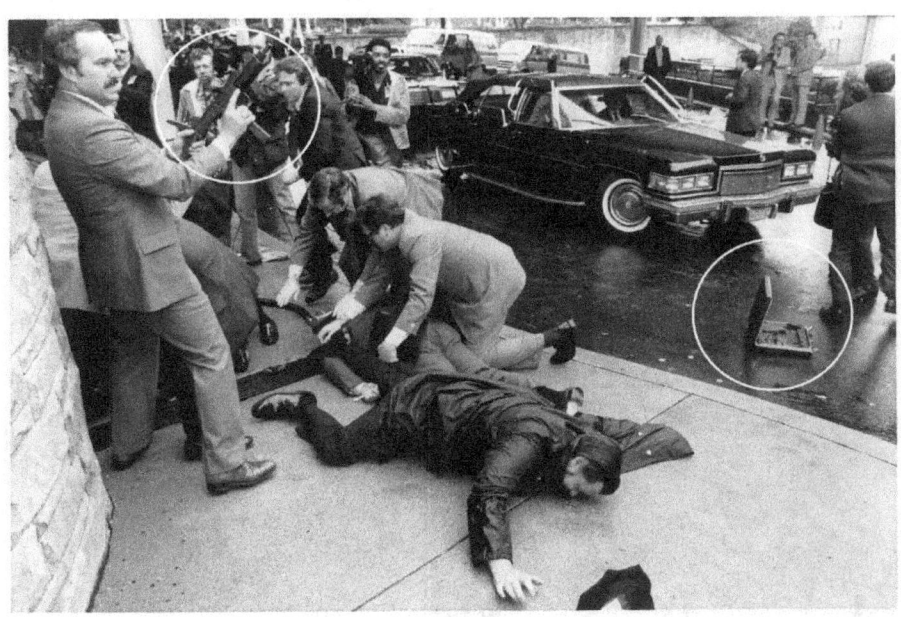

Figure 2. The same location perhaps 15 seconds later, after the shooting. The Secret Service has already restrained Hinckley. Notice the agent on the left holding the automatic weponry that has come out of the discarded case off to the right? The agent holding it is scanning for any more threats to "neutralize" as other agents take care of the President.

Terrorists are very unlikely to be able to get to Donald Trump while he is on the road. He has a very seasoned task force protecting him, with over a century of experience.

"Appreciate the congrats for being right on radical Islamic terrorism, I don't want congrats, I want toughness & vigilance. We must be smart!"

Donald J. Trump, June 12, 2016

06 Stretching the Secret Service Thin

At this point, some people may be quick to point out that reports leaking out of the Secret Service indicate that guarding Trump, and his jet-setting adult children, is massively straining the Secret Service staff and its budget. There are reports being generated that show the Herculean burden of protecting Donald Trump as he flies from vacation spot to vacation spot, and all of his rich children as they circumnavigate the globe in an attempt to promote the "Trump Inc." business empire, is wearing the Secret Service thin[2].

How massive is this additional drain of Secret Service resources? Current estimates are that it is costing 4 to 5 times as much to protect President Trump and his family than it did to protect President Barack Obama and his family.

The bill to protect president Obama and his family was nearly $97M. Rounded up, that is $12.5M per year. The price of Donald Trump's first three weekends has already cost over $10M.

Donald Trump is already costing the Secret Service in three weekends— just to protect him – almost as much as they had to expend to protect president Obama and his family for a full year.

Additionally, President Trump's weekly travel to his personal resort at Mar-a-Lago is straining agents as they must safeguard not merely the club and the entirety of the golf course he visits, they must also secure all of the island Mar-a-Lago sits on, and the surrounding waterways. That means Donald Trump's weekly jet-setting on Air Force One to play golf is not only a financial nightmare for US taxpayers, it is also a logistics and staffing nightmare for the Secret Service.

Let us ignore for the moment that Donald Trump swore up and down while he was campaigning that he would rarely ever leave the White House because he would be so busy working. Yes, it turns out that particular campaign promise was as reliable as everything else that comes out of Donald Trump's mouth. But a minority of Americans believed that lie enough to, along with the insanity of the Electoral College, make him President. That means that if he wants to fly back and forth between vacation spot and vacation spot, and send his children all over to promote his businesses, American taxpayers will just have to pay for it.

Furthermore, it is true that when the Secret Service gets stretched thin because the President treats Air Force One as his personal taxi service, it is far more likely that terrorists will be tempted to try and capitalize off of the situation.

That is a debate for another book.

This book seeks only to caution on the vulnerability of all of Donald Trump's soft targets in the form of his businesses and properties, and the fact that any human being directly at, or associated with, those properties are at a heightened risk of terrorist attack. Donald Trump could eliminate those vulnerabilities and risks simply by doing what every other ethical politician has done by placing their assets into a blind trust.

As such, the fact that the Secret Service has already stretched incredibly thin in protecting Trump and his family is irrelevant to the discussion of this book – except for one thing:

The fact that the Secret Service is already straining to protect President Trump and his family means that it is incredibly unlikely that it would expand its role and begin to protect the hundreds of Donald Trump properties, and the tens to hundreds of thousands of people that live, visit, and work in them.

Nor should it. Donald Trump is now in a position where he can treat the Department of Treasury as his own personal unlimited check book – but only so far as presidential matters go. When it comes to his personal assets – or his personal assets that he is currently pretending to allow his children to control – security of those is his personal burden.

"When you get these terrorists, you have to take out their families. They care about their lives, don't kid yourself. But they say they don't care about their lives. You have to take out their families."

Donald J. Trump, Dec 2, 2015

07 The Trump Targets!

Donald Trump has a weakness which is apparent to anyone who has heard him talk for more than roughly 15 to 20 seconds – he loves his money and showing off his wealth, and the Trump name his very public steady diet of Mammon. The man loves money and brazenly wallowing in it in a way that would make Scrooge McDuck vomit in disgust. He openly flaunts his opulent wealth in a way that makes one wonder if there is not a special circle in Dante's Inferno reserved just for Donald Trump. And perhaps most dangerously, he places his name on more of his tycoon toys than a 10-year-old with a label maker and six brothers and sisters.

The man loves his name.

Now, it is not unusual for rich and powerful men, and women, to place their names on their properties. It is an ego boost. It is a sign of power that alerts both rich and poor that this particular individual has reached a level that few can achieve.

But Donald Trump takes it to new extremes that dwarf even the hubris of Alexander the Great, who named at least 70 cities which he conquered, or created, "Alexandria".

Even the tyrant Joseph Stalin only had one Stalingrad.

Donald Trump has dozens of real properties that begin with the name, "Trump". He has hundreds of businesses named "Trump", which I will list – fully – later on. For terrorists who want to strike at America, would also like to hit the President of the United States, cause terror, and want what they consider to be the "glory of eternal recognition", these properties will be, and probably already are, key targets.

"We're led by a man that either is not tough, not smart, or he's got something else in mind... President Obama is acting the way he acts and can't even mention the words 'radical Islamic terrorism. There's something going on — it's inconceivable. There's something going on. He doesn't get it, or he gets it better than anybody understands. It's one or the other, and either one is unacceptable.

Donald J. Trump, June 13, 2016

08 Trump Tower – Trump's Crown Jewel and Prime Target

Figure 3. " All these trumped up towers, They're just golden showers...[3]"

Now, the Trump Tower in New York City that most people know of might be secure. Donald Trump lives there, and it is pretty certain that the Secret Service is keeping a fairly close eye on what goes on there. What that means is nobody is going to be getting on the elevator with Donald Trump unless they are specifically with Donald Trump. Nobody will be hacking the elevator and riding it up to Donald Trump's private suites. There will be no saran gas in the ventilation system, and no one will be sneaking in to the space underneath his living quarters to plant a bomb.

It is also a virtual certainty that by now the CIA, Secret Service, FBI, and NSA have thoroughly vetted each and every tenant in Trump Tower, and probably have scads of "listening devices" being monitored for even the slightest hint of subversive talk.

Figure 4. "Open to the Public"? President Trump's home is open to the public? Sigh...

It would surprise the hell out of me if every tenant of Trump Tower did not have their cell phones actively compromised by the United States Government with monitoring programs in place.

So in all likelihood the possibility of something happening to Donald Trump in Trump Tower is probably pretty low. As I said, the Secret Service members are professionals, and are highly dedicated to their jobs. Even if President Trump decides to sleep at a building that is technically "Open to the Public", that building is probably <u>very</u> secure.

But, how secure is that building when President Trump is not there? When he is scheduled away for a week or so, how many Secret Service agents are keeping the building, and the other tenants, safe?

Regardless of that number, this shows that Donald Trump the entity extends beyond Donald Trump the person. Because his assets are known and public, someone who wishes to hurt Donald Trump does not have to attack his person, or his family.

They can simply attack his assets.

And the Secret Service cannot protect them all.

"The media talks about home grown terrorism but Islamic radicalism and that's a very, very important term — a term that the president refuses to use and the networks that nurture it are imports from overseas whether you like it or whether you don't like it. Yes, there are many radicalized people already inside our country as a result of poor policies of the past."

Donald J. Trump, June 13, 2016

09 The Trump <u>Soft</u> Targets!

There are simply too many publicly known Donald Trump assets that are soft targets for terrorists to attack.

While the Secret Service undoubtedly keeps a tight rein on the Mar-a-Lago private country club were Donald Trump auctions off access to his person at the highest bidder, they do so only when the President is holding court there. It is not their job to protect that country club 24 hours a day 7 days a week for all 365 of the year. They are not there to watch every truck and every car coming into that ever-so-exclusive venue. They cannot inspect every box of goods delivered to make sure that none of them contain explosives, or chemical or biological weaponry.

Let's pull a page from an American-sponsored terrorist, shall we? Let's pull a page from the Tim McVeigh playbook. Here is a picture of the Alfred P. Murrah Federal Building before Tim McVeigh:

Figure 5. The front of the Alfred P. Murrah Federal Building, which allowed vehicles to park directly outside.

That building looks secure. It looks like you would need at least a tank and/or military grade heavy weaponry to cause it any serious harm. But here is a picture of it two days after Tim McVeigh parked outside:

Figure 6. The same building after Tim McVeigh capitalized off of the building's lax security measures. One terrorist did all of this with some fertilizer and a rented truck he parked a few feet away from the building's face.

How hard would it be for someone who wanted to get at the President to find a list of merchants that Mar-a-Lago does business with?

Not very.

How hard would it be for that person to get a delivery job with one of those merchants?

Probably not very hard – I suspect the turnover rate for delivery drivers that deliver ketchup, pesticide, or cracked crab[4] is quite high.

How hard would it be for that person to then substitute boxes of explosives instead of Heinz or shellfish, and drive them onto the Mar-a-Lago property and detonate them near dozens, or hundreds of guests?

You know the answer as well as I do – it would be easy. Incredibly easy. Terrorist do it in the Middle East all the time. It has happened in America dozens of times. All it takes is somebody with the will to do it. The Secret Service will not be there to intercept this delivery of death because the terrorist(s) will make this delivery at a time when the President is nowhere near Florida, and not scheduled to return for at least a week or two.

FAH-WHOOM!!! One large truck is turned into thousands of small pieces of shrapnel that tear through everything in their path that is softer than thick concrete. People? People's flesh barely slows down the flying hunks of sharp metal and glass.

Before the first ambulances arrive and begin to take shattered bodies to emergency rooms and morgues, the 24 hour a day news media are already streaming live feeds showing blood and destruction of Trump's business cronies at his private club for the mega rich. Law enforcement agencies will be left trying to piece together profile of whatever person or group of people did this horrible event as Donald Trump Tweets how this proves that his immigration ban was the right thing and would have prevented this tragedy... Even though it ultimately turns out that the person who drove the delivery vehicle was a US-born citizen and like most US terrorists, not Muslim.

Attendance at Mar-a-Lago plummets as his people quickly decide that they are safer in downtown Aleppo than at Trump's country club. Membership drops as people see no reason to spend a few hundred thousand dollars a year to be caught in the crossfire of a global struggle. Trump's reputation and wallet take massive hits. All of that, of course, only inspires others to, as the news media will call it, "copycat".

Except that it does not actually inspire copycat bombings. Nothing in this scenario is new. Over the past few decades it has played out dozens of times in America, and thousands of times across the globe. Indeed the first known use of a car bomb was one used in an assassination attempt on Sultan Abdul Hamid II in 1905. Every car bombing since then has been a "copycat" of that one, and that one is believed to be inspired by the Dutch use of "hellburner" ships against the Spanish in the 16th century.

Regardless of the fact that this hypothetical attack is hardly novel, the terrorist(s) which helped orchestrate this described attack have done massive damage to the President of the United States, achieved international recognition, and might someday very well be caught. But it does not matter if they are ever caught to the people that are dead. Those victims will have died because they were foolish enough to visit what is an obvious soft, and ever so inviting, target for terrorism. This is Donald Trump's private vacation getaway — he owns it. It is one of his favorite crown jewels[5]. The whole world knows he has set it up as his own palatial hall where he conducts business — and you might actually be able to bend his ear if you pay enough money to him for the privilege. Donald Trump's greed, Donald Trump's ego, and Donald Trump's stupidity have turned Mar-a-Lago into a most obvious and inviting target of terrorist attacks.

The fact we now have photos of him conducting (sort of) international emergency crisis management from the patio of his play toy property just further rings the dinner bell for salivating terrorists.

I am surprised an attack has not already happened there.

I am surprised that some whack-job paranoid hyper-progressive, or deranged dysfunctional anti-Communist has not been caught doing some impromptu attack on that property.

And here is a very beautiful question – because of the open and obvious value of Mar-a-Lago as a soft target for terrorism, shouldn't the comings and goings of every person and box of supplies that enter that property be searched as thoroughly as anyone or anything going into the White House?

Of course, the reality is that Donald Trump is not going to allow a moneymaking venture of his to be stained with such protections when he is not there because it might affect his bottom line. He did not want to place his assets in a blind trust because it might ultimately wind up costing him money. As a result of his refusal to do this, he has subjected US Citizens to a very real threat of terrorist attacks. Each and every one of his properties is a soft target for explosions. His bottled water – Trump Ice – is subject to being poisoned. His Miss Universe competitions, including the Miss Teen USA events down to the local level, are open season for an apolitical psycho like James Holmes to take a shotgun and blow away a few audience members and contestants.

Do not think something like that is likely to happen? John Hinckley shot President Reagan to get the attention of actress Jodie Foster – why not reverse it, and shoot a few beauty pageant contestants to get the attention of the President? Does anyone really think that some psychopath, sociopath, or self-titled "freedom fighter"—usually given a mandate by their "God"—has not already come up with the idea of attacking one of these pageants[6]?

Donald Trump cannot have it both ways. He cannot run on a platform screeching that America needs to end immigration into the country because of terrorist threats, and at the same time, place American citizens in harm's way for terrorist attacks because he does not want to lose a few dollars.

If terrorism is such a major threat that we must close US borders to refugees, then Donald Trump must bite the bullet and place his properties into a blind trust. His refusal to do so subjects every person that sets foot on one of his properties to the risk of a terrorist attack. Donald Trump is open and boastful about everything that he owns. He brags about it. He likes to emblaze his goodies with his name in big huge letters. If Donald Trump wants to risk damage to his own property, that is up to him. It is his property. If he wants to publish a list of 515 different commercial ventures that he owns for ISIS and Al Qaeda to simply print off of an Internet webpage and distribute to their operatives, that is up to him.

His property—let him waste it as he sees fit.

But his act of allowing anyone to go on to those properties when they are such an obvious and inviting soft target reeks of criminal recklessness. His refusal to place his properties into a blind trust, or otherwise liquidate them, shows that Donald Trump considers his pocketbook to be more valuable than the lives of the people that live in those properties, work in those properties, or visit those properties.

In a very real sense Donald Trump considers his bank account, and not losing a penny out of it, to be more valuable and important to him, than the life of your daughter – since your daughter could theoretically be competing in the Miss Teen competition for your state this year. He considers his opulent wealth, and not having it drop by a few percentage points, to be more important than the life of your son who is about to graduate from business school – since your son could be invited to play a round of golf at the Trump National Golf Club, Bedminster, New Jersey. Donald Trump considers his money to be more important than the lives of your mother and father – since they might visit the Cammack Retirement Group, one of several businesses housed in the 40 Wall Street Building, which is known as "The Trump Building".

Figure 7. 40 Wall Street, aka "The Trump Building". (Not to be confused with the dozens of other properties that bear his name like intentional crosshairs.)

Donald Trump does not care about your life, the lives of your loved ones, the lives of your family members, and the lives of your friends, business associates, casual acquaintances, people you distain, or even your blood enemies – none of those people matter in the least to him. By inviting you to come spend money at those properties while they are such potentially strong targets for terrorism, he is risking the lives of each and every person who steps near one of his properties by being the President of the United States while simultaneously keeping control of those hundreds of properties and companies which are such obvious targets for terrorism.

Yes, it is true that if he put them in a blind trust they might have lost somewhere between 5% to 8% of their value. Since Donald Trump claims to be worth $10 billion, and this might be the one time in his life when he is actually not lying[7], I am going to take him at his self-stated net worth of $10 billion. I am also going to raise the estimates for how much he might have lost in putting his assets into a blind trust up to 10%. That would mean that if Donald Trump had placed his assets into a blind trust his net worth would have dropped from $10 billion down to $9 billion. Yes, that is a significant amount of money to lose.

But Bill Gates has given away more money than that and somehow still gets by.

If Donald Trump's net worth dropped from $10 billion all the way down to the pitiful sum of $9 billion, I doubt he would notice it at all. He would still have other rich and poor people lining up and begging to be his newest sycophant, he would still have his free Twitter feed that he could use to attack people at 3 AM, and he could still afford to have whatever meal he wanted flown from whatever part of the world he wanted it flown from for every breakfast, lunch, dinner, and post-grope snack he whimed.

But Donald Trump does not want to give up any money, or power, in order to be President of the United States. And if that means you or your loved ones die as a result, he just does not care.

Not in the least.

"I'd say we've had a lot of problems with radical Islamic terrorism. That's what I'd say. We have a lot of problems. ... I'd say you've got to take a look at that, because something is going on. And it's not good."

Donald J. Trump, July 30, 2016

10 One Google Search Away

How public is Trump's list of properties? In years gone by, the mandatory Elections Commission filing that Trump did would have been buried somewhere that while technically public, would have been difficult for the average crackpot or mass murderer wannabe to get to. One would have had to file an official request in writing, wait the time period it took for the Government to get around to complying with their demand (if the person requesting it sent in the proper fee amount) and mail it back to them.

And there would have been a paper trail with at least some name the person requesting it was using, and at least a drop address that the FBI could look into.

Now? Now the amount of time it takes to find Trump assets and properties is one Google search away. Plus, your search is buried in with the thousands of other similar searches people did today. And buried with the ones done yesterday, and will be done tomorrow, and mixed in with others from all around the globe via whatever internet address faking relay people wish to use.

I decided to do a little test and Google "Donald Trump assets". One of the first search results was a Wikipedia entry listing Donald Trump owned businesses, with links to those individual entries. Clicking on the individual entries contained various entries of sub-organizations which Donald Trump owned. The Wikipedia entries were all very helpful, listing current and past Trump-owned businesses, along with address information, colorful high-resolution pictures, and various discussions on the aspects of the properties.

For some of these, I decided to do a little experiment — I then did a Google search for the tenants in some of the commercial buildings. Needless to say, Trump properties are very proud of the businesses that they lease space to, and finding lists of businesses that a terrorist could visit, seek employment at, or just send a package of weaponized Anthrax[8] to, were all there on the first page of the Google results.

Just by doing a few Google searches, and by going no farther than the second page of results, and no farther than two nestings deep into those results, here is the list of terrorism targets available for the laziest, and most slow-witted of terrorist wannabes and psychopathic attention seekers out there:

1) Miss Universe Organization
   a) Miss Teen USA
      i) Miss Teen USA state pageants
         (1) Miss Alabama Teen USA
         (2) Miss Alaska Teen USA
         (3) Miss Arizona Teen USA
         (4) Miss Arkansas Teen USA
         (5) Miss California Teen USA
         (6) Miss Colorado Teen USA
         (7) Miss Connecticut Teen USA
         (8) Miss Delaware Teen USA
         (9) Miss District of Columbia Teen USA
         (10) Miss Florida Teen USA
         (11) Miss Georgia Teen USA
         (12) Miss Hawaii Teen USA
         (13) Miss Idaho Teen USA
         (14) Miss Illinois Teen USA
         (15) Miss Indiana Teen USA
         (16) Miss Iowa Teen USA
         (17) Miss Kansas Teen USA
         (18) Miss Kentucky Teen USA
         (19) Miss Louisiana Teen USA
         (20) Miss Maine Teen USA
         (21) Miss Maryland Teen USA
         (22) Miss Massachusetts Teen USA

(23)Miss Michigan Teen USA

(24)Miss Minnesota Teen USA

(25)Miss Mississippi Teen USA

(26)Miss Missouri Teen USA

(27)Miss Montana Teen USA

(28)Miss Nebraska Teen USA

(29)Miss Nevada Teen USA

(30)Miss New Hampshire Teen USA

Figure 8, Will the Secret Service be there to protect these girls at all of their promotional events and appearances? No, they are on their own, and Trump does not care.

(31)Miss New Jersey Teen USA

(32)Miss New Mexico Teen USA

(33)Miss New York Teen USA

(34)Miss North Carolina Teen USA

(35)Miss North Dakota Teen USA

(36)Miss Ohio Teen USA

(37)Miss Oklahoma Teen USA

(38)Miss Oregon Teen USA

(39)Miss Pennsylvania Teen USA

(40)Miss Rhode Island Teen USA

(41)Miss South Carolina Teen USA

(42)Miss South Dakota Teen USA

(43)Miss Tennessee Teen USA

(44)Miss Texas Teen USA

(45)Miss Utah Teen USA

(46)Miss Vermont Teen USA

(47)Miss Virginia Teen USA

(48)Miss Washington Teen USA

(49)Miss West Virginia Teen USA

(50)Miss Wisconsin Teen USA

(51)Miss Wyoming Teen USA

b) Miss Universe

   i) Miss Universe National Pageants

     (1) Miss Universe Albania

     (2) Miss Algeria

     (3) Miss Antigua & Barbuda

     (4) Miss Argentina

     (5) Miss Universe Australia

     (6) Miss Azerbaijan

     (7) Miss Universe Bahamas

     (8) Miss Bahrain

     (9) Miss Bénin

     (10)Miss Universe Botswana

     (11)Miss Universo Brasil

     (12)Miss British Virgin Islands

     (13)Miss National Team Bulgaria

     (14)Miss Universe Canada

     (15)Miss Cayman Islands

     (16)Miss Universe China

     (17)Miss Colombia

     (18)Miss Cook Islands

     (19)Miss Costa Rica

     (20)Miss Universe Croatia

     (21)Miss Cuba

(22)Czech Miss

(23)Face of Denmark

(24)Miss Universe Denmark

(25)Miss Dominican Republic

(26)Miss Estonia

(27)Miss Ethiopia

(28)Miss Universe Ethiopia

(29)Miss Gabon

(30)Miss Gambia

(31)Miss Universe Germany

(32)Miss Universe Ghana

(33)Star Hellas

(34)Miss Guam

(35)Miss Guyana

(36)Miss Haiti

(37)Miss Honduras

(38)Miss Universe Hungary

(39)Miss Universe Ireland

(40)Miss Israel

(41)Miss Jamaica Universe

(42)Miss International Japan

(43)Miss Universe Japan

(44)Miss Kazakhstan

(45)Miss Universe Kenya

(46)Miss Universe Korea

(47)Miss Kurdistan

(48)Miss Kyrgyzstan

(49)Miss Laos

(50)Miss Universe Latvia

(51)Miss Universe Malaysia

(52)Miss Estrella Mauritius

(53)Nuestra Belleza México

(54)Señorita México

(55)Miss Belgium

(56)Miss Trinidad and Tobago

(57)Miss Trinidad and Tobago Universe

(58)Miss Universe Japan 2015

(59)Miss Universe Sweden

(60)Miss Maroc

(61)Miss Myanmar

(62)Miss Namibia

(63)Miss Nederland

(64)Miss Nederland Universe

(65)Miss Universe New Zealand

(66)Miss Norway

(67)Miss Polonia

(68)Miss República Portuguesa

(69)Miss St. Martin

(70)Miss Samoa

(71)Miss Universe Sierra Leone

(72)Miss Singapore Universe

(73)Miss Universe Slovenskej Republiky

(74)Miss RSA

(75)Miss South Africa

(76)Miss Spain

(77)Miss Universe Sri Lanka

(78)Miss St. Lucia

(79)Miss Suriname

(80)Miss Universe Tanzania

(81)Miss Universe Thailand

(82)Miss Turks and Caicos

(83)Miss Ukraine Universe

(84)Miss US Virgin Islands

(85)Miss Universe Zambia

(86)Miss Zimbabwe

c) Miss USA

    i) Miss USA State Pageants

        (1) Miss Alabama USA

        (2) Miss Alaska USA

(3) Miss Arizona USA

(4) Miss Arkansas USA

(5) Miss California USA

(6) Miss Colorado USA

(7) Miss Connecticut USA

(8) Miss Delaware USA

(9) Miss District of Columbia USA

(10) Miss Florida USA

(11) Miss Georgia USA

(12) Miss Hawaii USA

(13) Miss Idaho USA

(14) Miss Illinois USA

(15) Miss Indiana USA

(16) Miss Iowa USA

Figure 9. How well guarded are all of the Miss USA pageants and their practices? All it takes is for one person with bad intentions to sneak through as a guest or worker.

(17) Miss Kansas USA

(18) Miss Kentucky USA

(19) Miss Louisiana USA

(20) Miss Maine USA

(21) Miss Maryland USA

(22) Miss Massachusetts USA

(23) Miss Michigan USA

(24)Miss Minnesota USA

(25)Miss Mississippi USA

(26)Miss Missouri USA

(27)Miss Montana USA

(28)Miss Nebraska USA

(29)Miss Nevada USA

(30)Miss New Hampshire USA

(31)Miss New Jersey USA

(32)Miss New Mexico USA

(33)Miss New York USA

(34)Miss North Carolina USA

(35)Miss North Dakota USA

(36)Miss Ohio USA

(37)Miss Oklahoma USA

(38)Miss Oregon USA

(39)Miss Pennsylvania USA

(40)Miss Rhode Island USA

(41)Miss South Carolina USA

(42)Miss South Dakota USA

(43)Miss Tennessee USA

(44)Miss Texas USA

(45)Miss Utah USA

(46)Miss Vermont USA

(47)Miss Virginia USA

(48)Miss Washington USA

(49)Miss West Virginia USA

(50)Miss Wisconsin USA

(51)Miss Wyoming USA

2) Trump Productions
   a) The Apprentice
   b) The Celebrity Apprentice

3) Central Park Carousel (Trump Carousel)

Figure 10. The quaint Trump Carousel, where children and lovers ride...

a) The Central Park Carousel is a vintage carousel located in Central Park in Manhattan, New York City, at the southern end of the park, near East 65th Street.

b) Part of the New York City Landmarks Preservation Commission's Central Park Scenic Landmarks.

Figure 11. Donald Trump is famous in NYC for having saved this attraction.

4) Mar-a-Lago

Figure 12. Mar-a-Lago. Donald Trump's private Royal Court where you are not invited (unless you give The Donald a few hundred thousand to join, of course) and Government open records laws do not apply.

a) The 126-room, 110,000-square-foot (10,000 m2) house contains the Mar-a-Lago Club, a members-only. The Trump family maintains private quarters in a separate, closed-off area of the house and grounds. [9]

Figure 13. The closest YOU will ever get to seeing the inside of Mar-a-Lago. Here Tycoon Trump poses with a friend. (Her image was blurred to protect her identity.)

5) The Old Post Office Pavilion

Figure 14. Trump's Old Post Office Pavilion. Notice the fact anyone can park right outside of it, or crash a bomb-laden truck right through the entrance? Now go back and look at the pictures of the front of the Alfred P. Murrah Federal Building.

a) The Old Post Office Pavilion, historically known as the Old Post Office and Clock Tower, located at 1100 Pennsylvania Avenue NW in Washington, D.C.

b) Trump developed the property into a luxury hotel, Trump International Hotel Washington, D.C. which opened in September 2016.

c) Tenants[10]:

   i)   Bagel Express

   ii) Ben and Jerry's

   iii) Enrico's Pizza

iv) Everything Yogurt

v) Georgetown Deli

vi) Greek Taverna

vii) Indian Delight

viii) Panda Café

ix) Sushi Shogun

x) Alamo Flags

xi) Collectables

xii) Finishing Touch

xiii) Larry's Cookies

xiv) Short Stop News

xv) Sonya's Leather

6) 40 Wall Street (The Trump Building – see image above)

a) 40 Wall Street, also known as the Trump Building, is a 71-story skyscraper in New York City. (See image above)

b) According to 2015 Federal Election Commission filings, Trump has an outstanding mortgage on the property in excess of $50 million.[18]

c) As of 2009, Country-Wide Insurance Company was the single largest tenant at 40 Wall Street, having made it its home since 1998.

i) Tenants[11]

(1) Access Intelligence

(2) ACI/ Gettenberg

(3) American Precious Metals Exchange (APMEX)

(4) Bay Crest Partners

(5) Boyce Technologies

(6) Brokerage & Management

(7) Camacho Mauro Mullholland

(8) Cammack Retirement Group

(9) China Investment Federation

(10) Coastal Trading Securities

(11) Core Staffing Services

(12) Countrywide Insurance Services

(13)Dean & DeLuca

(14)Direct Access Partners

(15)Duane Reade

(16)Elite Brands

(17)Euroclear Bank

(18)Extech Solutions

(19)First Investors

(20)Foran Glennon

(21)Frank Xu and Caay Institute

(22)GDS Publishing

(23)Girl Scouts of America

(24)Global Alliance for TB Drug Development

(25)Grandfield & Dodd

(26)Green Ivy

(27)Hadassah

(28)HAKS

(29)Haks Engineers

(30)Halperin Battaglia Raicht

(31)Harris, O'Brien, St. Laurent & Chaudry

(32)Harry Fox Agency

(33)Hidrock Realty

(34)Huron Consulting Services

(35)IBIS

(36)IBISWorld

(37)ICF International

(38)ID Matters

(39)Infinitel

(40)Jajan

(41)JH Darbie & Co.

(42)Kelly & Rubin

(43)Lane McVicker

(44)Leeds & Leeds

(45)Leslie E. Robertson Associates (LERA)

(46)Magna Group Capital

(47)MASS Communications

(48)Mercury Media

(49)Milk Street Café

(50)N. Cheng & Co.

(51)N. Cheng CPA

(52)Newman Myers Kreines Gross Harris

(53)NFP Property & Casualty Services

(54)NYG Capital

(55)Office Space Solutions

(56)P&B Partners

(57)Park Jensen Bennett

(58)Paulson Investment Company

(59)Piyi Investment

(60)Public Financial Management

(61)RCL Associates

(62)Reliance Capital Group & Empire America Holdings

(63)RG Michaels

(64)Rosabianca & Associates

(65)Rosenblatt Securities

(66)RRZ Investment Management

(67)SNC Investments

(68)Sojitz Corporation of America

(69)SS&C Technologies

(70)Synergenics

(71)Tachless International

(72)Telstraorporated

(73)The Judge Group

(74)United Advisors

(75)Weidlinger Associates

(76)Xcitek Solutions Plus

(77)XO Communications

(78)Zaremba Brownell & Brown

7) Trump Fragrances
   a) As of November 8, 2016, all of Trump's fragrances are reported to be in the process of being discontinued.[12]
8) Trump Home
   a) Trump Home is a brand of furniture and home items
9) Trump Ice, also known as Trump Natural Spring Water
10) Golf Courses
   a) Trump International Golf Club, West Palm Beach is a private 27 hole golf course in West Palm Beach, Florida.

Figure 15. Trump knows that if security is beefed up too much in places like this, membership will fall.

   b) Trump National Golf Resort Doral Miami is a golf resort in Doral in south Florida in the United States.

Figure 16. Trump National Golf Resort Doral Miami

   c) Trump National Golf Club, Bedminster is a private golf club in Bedminster, New Jersey.

   d) Trump National Golf Club, Los Angeles is a public golf club in Rancho Palos Verdes, California

   e) Trump National Golf Club (Philadelphia) is a private golf club located in Pine Hill, New Jersey

   f) Trump National Golf Club, Washington, D.C. is an 800-acre private golf club at Lowes Island in Potomac Falls, Virginia

   g) Trump National Golf Club Westchester is a private golf club in Briarcliff Manor, New York

   h) Trump Turnberry
      i) is a golf resort on the coast of the outer Firth of Clyde in southwestern Scotland

   i) The Trump National Golf Club Colts Neck

11) The Trump International Hotel and Towers

   a) Trump International Hotel and Tower (Chicago)

   b) Trump International Hotel and Tower (Honolulu)

   c) Trump International Hotel and Tower (New York City)

   d) Trump International Hotel and Tower (Toronto)

   e) Trump International Hotel and Tower (Vancouver)

f) Trump International Hotel Las Vegas
g) Trump International Hotel Washington, D.C. a.k.a. Old Post Office Pavilion
h) Trump Ocean Club International Hotel and Tower, in Panama City

12) Trump Model Management.
a) Trump Model Management is a New York City-based modeling agency, founded in 1999.
b) Was where Melania worked when she met Donald Trump.

Figure 17. Melania AFTER she stopped working illegally in the US. I guess Donald doesn't mind ALL illegal foreign workers stealing jobs from Americans...

14) Trump Park Avenue
   a) Trump Park Avenue is a former skyscraper hotel converted to a residential condominium
   b) 120 luxury condominium apartments and 8 penthouses.

Figure 18. Trump Park Avenue. Last year, a condominium building terrorists would not have looked twice at. But his year...? All bets are off.

15) Trump Plaza (also known as Trump Plaza Residences)
   a) 445 units. It is the tallest residential building in New Jersey

Figure 19. The not-quite-attractive Trump Plaza.

17) Trump Steaks
   a) West Palm Beach Florida
      i) Steaks are actually a private labeling of Steaks from Bush Brothers Provision Co., in West Palm Beach, Florida[13]
18) Trump Wine
   a) Handed over to Eric
   b) Website says, ""Trump Winery is a registered trade name of Eric Trump Wine Manufacturing LLC, which is not owned, managed or affiliated with Donald J. Trump, The Trump Organization or any of their affiliates."
19) Trump Tower
   a) Insane to go in there.
   b) Trump Tower is a 58-story, 664-foot-high (202 m) mixed-use skyscraper located at 721–725 Fifth Avenue between 56th and 57th Streets in Midtown Manhattan, New York City
   c) Trump Tower serves as the headquarters for The Trump Organization and houses the penthouse condominium residence of U.S. President Donald Trump.
   d) Tenants[14]
      i) Asprey
      ii) B&B Investments
      iii) Concord International Investments
      iv) European School of Economics
      v) Gucci
      vi) Industrial and Commercial Bank of China
      vii) International School of NY
      viii) Lightfoot Capital
      ix) Marc Fisher Shoes
      x) Qatar Airways
20) Trump Tower Manila
   a) Trump Tower Manila, also known as Trump Tower at Century City, is a residential building located in Makati, Metro Manila, Philippines
   b) Construction was nearly finished as of November 2016

21) The Trump International Hotel and Tower Vancouver
   a) A skyscraper in Downtown Vancouver, British Columbia, Canada. The 69-story, 187.8 meters (616 ft), mixed-use tower is located at 1151 West Georgia Street, and was completed in 2016.
22) Wollman Rink

Figure 20. Donald Trump is famous in NYC for having also saved this Central Park Attraction.

   a) Wollman Rink is a public ice rink in the southern part of Central Park, Manhattan, New York City.
23) Trump's Helicopters
24) Sentient Jets, LLC (Trump Jets LLC)

And at this point, we simply start to pull from the Financial Disclosure Forms. All information you would ever want about these properties is online, for any terrorist to read. For convenience sake, I will only list businesses and other properties that contain the name "Trump" in them.

25) Financial Disclosure forms[15]
- a) 515 Listed with detailed information
- b) 286 Companies bear Trump's Name, with additional properties also bearing his name.
    - i) Sentient Jets LLC (Now/Known/As Trump Jets LLC)
    - ii) T International Realty LLC (dba Trump International Realty)
    - iii) The Donald J. Trump Foundation, Inc.
    - iv) The Trump Corporation
    - v) The Trump Follies Member Inc.
    - vi) The Trump Equitable Fifth Avenue Company
    - vii) Trump 106 CPS LLC
    - viii) Trump 55 Wall Corp
    - ix) Trump 767 Management LLC
    - x) Trump 845 LP LLC
    - xi) Trump 845 UN GP LLC
    - xii) Trump 846 UN MGR Corp
    - xiii) Trump 846 UN MGR LLC fka 845 UN LLC
    - xiv) Trump AC Casino Marks LLC
    - xv) Trump AC Casino Marks Member Corp
    - xvi) Trump Acquisition Corp.
    - xvii) Trump Acquisition, LLC
    - xviii) Trump Books LLC
    - xix) Trump Books Manager Corp
    - xx) Trump Brazil LLC
    - xxi) Trump Briarcliff Manor Development LLC formerly Briar Hall Development LLC
    - xxii) Trump Canadian Services Inc
    - xxiii) Trump Canouan Estate LLC
    - xxiv) Trump Canouan Estate Member Corp
    - xxv) Trump Caribbean LLC
    - xxvi) Trump Carousel LLC

xxvii)   Trump Carousel Member Corp

xxviii)   Trump Central Park West Corp

xxix)   Trump Chicago Commercial Member Corp

xxx)   Trump Chicago Commercial Manager LLC

xxxi)   Trump Chicago Development LLC

xxxii)   Trump Chicago Hotel Member Corp

xxxiii)   Trump Chicago Hotel Manager LLC

xxxiv)   Trump Chicago Managing Member LLC

xxxv)   Trump Chicago Member LLC

xxxvi)   Trump Chicago Residential Member Corp

xxxvii)   Trump Chicago Residential Manager LLC

xxxviii)   Trump Chicago Retail LLC

xxxix)   Trump Chicago Retail Manager LLC

xl)   Trump Chicago Retail Member Corp

xli)   Trump Classic Cars LLC

xlii)   Trump Classic Cars Member Corp

xliii)   Trump Commercial Chicago LLC

xliv)   Trump Cozumel Corp

xlv)   Trump Cozumel LLC

xlvi)   Trump CPS Corp

xlvii)   Trump CPS LLC

xlviii)   Trump Delmonico LLC

xlix)   Trump Development Services LLC

l)   Trump Development Services Member Corp.

li)   Trump Drinks Israel Holdings LLC

lii)   Trump Drinks Israel Holdings Member Corp

liii)   Trump Drinks Israel LLC

liv)   Trump Drinks Israel Member Corp

lv)   Trump Education ULC

lvi)   Trump Empire State, Inc.

lvii)   Trump Endeavor 12 LLC

lviii)   Trump Endeavor 12 Manager Corp

lix)   Trump EU Marks Member LLC

lx)   Trump EU Marks Member Corp

lxi)   The Trump Entrepreneur Initiative LLC (fka Trump University CA LLC)

lxii)   Trump Ferry Point LLC

lxiii)   Trump Ferry Point Member Corp

lxiv)   Trump Florida Management LLC

lxv)   Trump Florida Manager Corp.

lxvi)   The Trump Follies LLC

lxvii)   Trump Fort Lee LLC

lxviii)   Trump Fort Lee Member Corp

lxix)   Trump Golf Acquisition LLC

lxx)   Trump Golf Coco Beach LLC

lxxi)   Trump Golf Coco Beach Member Corp

lxxii)   Trump Golf Management LLC

lxxiii)   Trump Home Marks

lxxiv)   Trump Home Marks Member Corp

lxxv)   Trump Ice LLC

lxxvi)   Trump Ice Inc

lxxvii)   Trump Identity LLC

lxxviii) Trump Identity Member Corp

lxxix)   Trump International Development LLC

lxxx)   Trump International Development Member Corp

lxxxi)   Trump International Golf Club LC

lxxxii)   Trump International Golf Club Scotland Limited

lxxxiii) Trump International Golf Club Inc.

lxxxiv)   Trump International Hotel and Tower Condominium

lxxxv)   Trump International Hotel Hawaii LLC

lxxxvi)   Trump International Hotels Management LLC

lxxxvii) Trump International Management Corp

lxxxviii) Trump Kelowna LLC

lxxxix)   Trump Kelowna Member Corp.

xc)   Trump Korean Projects LLC

xci)   Trump Las Olas LLC

xcii)   Trump Las Olas Member Corp

xciii)   Trump Las Vegas Corp.

xciv)	Trump Las Vegas Development LLC
xcv)	Trump Las Vegas Managing Member LLC
xcvi)	Trump Las Vegas Managing Member II LLC
xcvii)	Trump Las Vegas Marketing and Sales LLC
xcviii)	Trump Las Vegas Member LLC
xcix)	Trump Las Vegas Member II LLC
c)	Trump Las Vegas Sales & Marketing Inc.
ci)	Trump International Hotel & Tower Las Vegas Unit Owners Association
cii)	Trump Lauderdale Development 2 LLC
ciii)	Trump Lauderdale Development LLC
civ)	Trump Management Inc
cv)	Trump Marketing LLC
cvi)	Trump Marks Asia Corp
cvii)	Trump Marks Asia LLC
cviii)	Trump Marks Atlanta LLC
cix)	Trump Marks Atlanta Member Corp
cx)	Trump Marks Baja Corp
cxi)	Trump Marks Baja LLC
cxii)	Trump Marks Batumi LLC
cxiii)	Trump Marks Batumi Member Corp
cxiv)	Trump Marks Beverages Corp
cxv)	Trump Marks LLC
cxvi)	Trump Marks Canouan Corp
cxvii)	Trump Marks Canouan LLC
cxviii)	Trump Marks Chicago LLC
cxix)	Trump Marks Chicago Member Corp
cxx)	Trump Marks Cozumel Corp
cxxi)	Trump Marks Cozumel LLC
cxxii)	Trump Marks Dubai Corp
cxxiii)	Trump Marks Dubai LLC
cxxiv)	Trump Marks Egypt Corp
cxxv)	Trump Marks Egypt LLC
cxxvi)	Trump Marks Fine Foods LLC
cxxvii)	Trump Marks Fine Foods Member Corp

cxxviii)   Trump Marks Ft. Lauderdale LLC
cxxix)   Trump Marks Ft. Lauderdale Member Corp
cxxx)   Trump Marks Golf Swing LLC
cxxxi)   Trump Marks Golf Swing Member Corp
cxxxii)   Trump Marks GP Corp
cxxxiii)   Trump Marks Holding LP (FKA Trump Marks LP)
cxxxiv)   Trump Marks Hollywood Corp
cxxxv)   Trump Marks Hollywood LLC
cxxxvi)   Trump Marks Istanbul II Corp.
cxxxvii)   Trump Marks Istanbul II LLC
cxxxviii)   Trump Marks Jersey City Corp.
cxxxix)   Trump Marks Jersey City LLC
cxl)   Trump Marks Las Vegas Corp
cxli)   Trump Marks Las Vegas LLC
cxlii)   Trump Marks LLC
cxliii)   Trump Marks Magazine Corp
cxliv)   Trump Marks Magazine LLC
cxlv)   Trump Marks Mattress LLC
cxlvi)   Trump Marks Mattress Member Corp.
cxlvii)   Trump Marks Menswear LLC
cxlviii)   Trump Marks Menswear Member Corp
cxlix)   Trump Marks Mortoaoe Corp.
cl)   Trump Marks Mtg LLC
cli)   Trump Marks Mumbai LLC
clii)   Trump Marks Mumbai Member Corp
cliii)   Trump Marks New Orleans Corp
cliv)   Trump Marks New Orleans LLC
clv)   Trump Marks New Rochelle Corp.
clvi)   Trump Marks New Rochelle LLC
clvii)   Trump Marks Palm Beach Corp
clviii)   Trump Marks Palm Beach LLC
clix)   Trump Marks Panama Corp
clx)   Trump Marks Panama LLC
clxi)   Trump Marks Philadelphia Corp

clxii)   Trump Marks PhiladelPhia LLC

clxiii)   Trump Marks Philippines LLC

clxiv)   Trump Marks Phil ippine s Corp

clxv)   Trump Marks Products LLC

clxvi)   Trump Marks Products Member Corp

clxvii)   Trump Marks Puerto Rico I LLC

clxviii)   Trump Marks Puerto Rico I Member Corp

clxix)   Trump Marks Puerto Rico II LLC

clxx)   Trump Marks Puerto Rico II Member Corp

clxxi)   Trump Marks Punta del Este LLC

clxxii)   Trump Marks Punta del Este Manager Corp

clxxiii)   The Donald J. Trump Company LLC

clxxiv)   The Trump Marks Real Estate Corp

clxxv)   Trump Marks Real Estate LLC

clxxvi)   Trump Marks SOHO License Corp

clxxvii)   Trump Marks SOHO LLC

clxxviii)   Trump Marks South Africa LLC

clxxix)   Trump Marks South Africa Member Corp

clxxx)   Trump Marks Stamford Corp

clxxxi)   Trump Marks Stamford LLC

clxxxii)   Trump Marks Sunny Isles I LLC

clxxxiii)   Trump Marks Sunny Isles I Member Corp.

clxxxiv)   Trump Marks Sunny Isles II LLC

clxxxv)   Trump Marks Sunny Isles II Member Corp.

clxxxvi)   Trump Marks Tampa Corp

clxxxvii)   Trump Marks Tampa LLC

clxxxviii) Trump Marks Toronto Corp

clxxxix)   Trump Marks Toronto LLC

cxc)   Trump Marks Toronto LP (formally Trump Toronto Management LP)

cxci)   Trump Marks Waikiki Corp

cxcii)   Trump Marks Waikiki LLC

cxciii)   Trump Marks Westchester Corp.

cxciv)   Trump Marks Westchester LLC

cxcv)   Trump Marks White Plains Corp

cxcvi)	Trump Marks White Plains LLC
cxcvii)	Trump Miami Resort Management LLC
cxcviii)	Trump Miami Resort Management Member Corp
cxcix)	Trump National Golf Club Colts Neck LLC
cc)	Trump National Golf Club Colts Neck Member Corp
cci)	Trump National Golf Club LLC
ccii)	Trump National Golf Club Member Corp
cciii)	Trump National Golf Club Washington DC LLC
cciv)	Trump National Golf Club Washington DC Member Corp
ccv)	Trump Ocean Manager Inc.
ccvi)	Trump Ocean Managing Member LLC
ccvii)	Trump Old Post Office LLC
ccviii)	Trump On the Ocean LLC
ccix)	Trump Organization LLC
ccx)	The Trump Organization, Inc.
ccxi)	Trump Pageants, Inc.
ccxii)	Trump Palace Condominium
ccxiii)	Trump Palace/Parc LLC
ccxiv)	Trump Panama Condominium Management LLC
ccxv)	Trump Panama Condominium Member Corp
ccxvi)	Trump Panama Hotel Management LLC
ccxvii)	Trump Panama Hotel Management Member Corp LLC
ccxviii)	Trump Parc East Condominium
ccxix)	Trump Park Avenue Acquisition LLC
ccxx)	Trump Park Avenue LLC
ccxxi)	Trump Payroll Chicago LLC
ccxxii)	Trump Payroll Corp.
ccxxiii)	Trump Phoenix Development LLC
ccxxiv)	Trump Plaza LLC
ccxxv)	Trump Plaza Member Inc. fka Trump Plaza Corp.
ccxxvi)	Trump Procida Fort Lee LLC
ccxxvii)	Trump Productions LLC (former Rancho Lien LLC)
ccxxviii)	Trump Production Managing Member Inc
ccxxix)	Trump Project Management Corp.

ccxxx) Trump Properties LLC

ccxxxi) Trump Realty Services, LLC (fka Trump Mortgage Services LLC (03) & Tower Mortgage Services LLC)

ccxxxii) Trump Restaurants LLC

ccxxxiii) Trump RHF Corp

ccxxxiv) Trump Riverside Management LLC

ccxxxv) Trump Ruffin Commercial LLC

ccxxxvi) Trump Ruffin LLC

ccxxxvii) Trump Ruffin Tower I LLC

ccxxxviii) Trump Sales & Leasing Chicago LLC

ccxxxix) Trump Sales & Leasing Chicago Member Corp

ccxl) Trump Scotland Member Inc

ccxli) Trump Scotsborough Square LLC

ccxlii) Trump Scotsborough Square Member Corp.

ccxliii) Trump SoHo Hotel Condominium New York

ccxliv) Trump Soho Member LLC

ccxlv) Trump Toronto Development Inc

ccxlvi) Trump Toronto Hotel Management Corp.

ccxlvii) Trump Toronto Member Corp. (formaly Trump Toronto Management Member Corp)

ccxlviii) Trump Tower Commercial LLC

ccxlix) Trump Tower Condominium Residential Section

ccl) Trump Tower Managing Member Inc

ccli) Trump Village Construction Corp.

cclii) Trump Vineyard Estates LLC

ccliii) Trump Vineyard Estates Manager Corp.

ccliv) Trump Vineyard Estates Lot 3 Owner LLC (fka Eric Trump Land Holdings LLC)

cclv) Trump Virginia Acquisitions LLC (fka Virginia Acquisitions LLC)

cclvi) Trump Virginia Acquisitions Manager Corp

cclvii) Trump Virginia Lot 5 LLC

cclviii) Trump Virginia Lot 5 Manager Corp.

cclix) Trump Wine Marks LLC

cclx) Trump Wine Marks Member Corp.

cclxi)	Trump World Productions LLC y LLC
cclxii)	Trump World Productions Manager Corp
cclxiii)	Trump World Publications LLC
cclxiv)	Trump/New World Property Management LLC
cclxv)	Trump Castle Management Corp
cclxvi)	Trump Marks White Plains Corp
cclxvii)	Trump RHF Corp
cclxviii)	The Donald J. Trump grantor Trust – DJT is the Trustee Successor – Trustee is Donald J. Trump, Jr.
cclxix)	The Donald J. Trump Revocable Trust

"Our jobs have moved overseas, Islamic terrorism has spread within our shores and an open border has crushed low-income workers and threatened our security."

Donald J. Trump, August 24, 2016

11 Trump's Name INVITES Terrorism

Wow... Just... Wow. Donald Trump's wallet is surpassed only by Donald Trump's ego – over half of the businesses he owns bear his name. Now, in fairness, there is a strong argument to be made that his name carries with it name recognition. That means that slapping his name on an investment ultimately helps the investment succeed because people automatically know that said investment is associated with Donald Trump – the rich billionaire.

But won't the terrorists know the exact same thing? Will not they automatically know that striking at any property showcased with the word "Trump" will automatically mean international recognition for having attacked President Trump directly? Indeed, even if nobody was injured in an attack on the Trump Carousel, wouldn't a Centennial Olympic Park style bombing on that property send massive shock waves through the news media? Wouldn't such an attack seriously hurt Donald Trump's finances as tenants wise up and leave his properties?

When a foreign power that actively sponsors state-run terrorism decides to do a sequel to the Boston Marathon Bombing, which of the Miss Teen USA pageants will they target?

Idaho? Georgia? New York?

Why not simply tamper with a domestic product like Melania Trump's cosmetic line? The person who did that with Tylenol back in 1982 was never caught, and that means any low-level domestic sociopath could easily contaminate a large amount of those cosmetics.

How long until a ship carrying the Trump signature line of business attire sewn in Asian sweatshops at $1.30 an hour is blown up in Los Angeles harbor?

And Donald Trump just does not care. It will not be his blood that is spilled, so he is gambling with the lives of everyone who lives in, works at, or visits any Trump properties. The man is not an idiot – he might be a tyrant, a huckster, a megalomaniac, and a fraud, but he is not an idiot. He might be shortsighted when it comes to his own limitations in thinking he can run America as he would his own private company, but he is not stupid. He knows that every single property I have listed is subject to attacks.

But he does not care that everybody who visits any one of his properties, unlike him with his legions of Secret Service details, are all incredibly soft targets.

Figure 21. The Boston Marathon Bombing. This event was chosen for the name recognition of the event--the bigger the name, the more it gets recognized. Wouldn't anything bearing the Trump name invite attacks even more?

There are those people that will argue that terrorists do not care about name recognition – that terrorists just want to kill as many people as possible. It is true that some terrorists probably just want a high body count, and to them killing 50 people at a non-Trump property is more desirable than killing 25 people at a Trump property. But the very word "terrorism" comes from committing acts which inspire terror in others.

What that means is the greater the name recognition of the target, the greater the likelihood that the terrorist act achieves what the terrorists wanted.

Don't believe me?

The picture I just gave you of the Boston Marathon Bombing is an event that I am sure a vast majority of readers will remember. In that attack, a total of three people were killed. That attack gathered more media attention than the Orlando shooting. Right now, some of you are struggling to remember what the Orlando shooting was. Some people will remember it as the ISIS-related or inspired shooting that took place in Orlando Florida where 49 people were killed.

The Boston Marathon Bombing killed 3 people. The shooting in the Pulse nightclub killed 49. Yet more people are more likely to remember the details of the Boston Marathon Bombing because of the fact that they were already familiar with the Boston Marathon. Attacking something people were already familiar with guarantees that the terrorist attack will get lodged in the national psyche, and receive lots of press coverage.

Now imagine the national hysteria and voracious appetites of the 24-hour news media, blogosphere, and pundits on both sides after the first Trump property – of whatever nature – is brought down by terrorism.

Not only will Donald Trump suffer directly from this first of possibly many attacks, but the terrorist will undoubtedly lose no sleep over the fact that they have harmed and killed US citizens that helped put Trump into office.

"*I have a message for the terrorists trying to kill our citizens: we will find you, we will destroy you, and we will win. This is not only a military fight, but we will also require cyberwarfare and financial warfare. It is also an ideological fight. We will confront directly the hateful ideology of Radical Islam — and promote American values, and American culture, and America's system of government.*

Donald J. Trump, August 24, 2016

12 How Terrorists Choose Their Targets

At this point, I feel it is important to discuss how terrorists – whether international or domestic – choose their targets. There has been much research done on this subject, and sadly the best that can be gleaned from comprehensive studies is a mishmash of generalities. There are certain statistics which can be gathered from studying terrorist acts such as the fact that 44% of all terrorists lived within 30 miles of their targets, or that international style terrorists tended to live close to their targets, while domestic terrorists tended to be rural living but choose targets in nearby cities.

While some trends can be discerned from these studies, the problem is that while we tend to think of "terrorists" as a singular strain of monsters, the reality is much more complex. Terrorists come from all religions, all socioeconomic groups, all educational backgrounds, and all political philosophies. Because of the difficulties which America is facing with Islamic terrorism, we tend to think of terrorism as being primarily done by Muslims on non-Muslims.

However according to the FBI Database[16], when looking at all terror attacks on US soil from 1980 to 2005, the breakdown was:

5% were carried out by Communists
6% were carried out by Islamic Extremists
7% were carried out by Jewish Extremists
24% were carried out by extreme left-wing groups
42% were carried out by Latinos
16% were carried out by "other"

The largest group, "Latino", appears to be misplaced, because Latino is not a specific ideology, religion, or political group. While generalizations can be made, such as they tend to be for more relaxed immigration rules, or they tend to be Catholic, those are very broad generalizations, and do not specifically lend themselves to being a basis for terrorist activities.

Thus it appears that Latino does not really belong as a category in the group of "terrorists".

But the reality is that that singular group "Latino" illustrates the problem with America's view on terrorism. Terrorism is not from religion. It is not from a political party. It is not from wealth, or lack thereof. It is not from where you were born. It is not from educational level.

Terrorism is the actualization of the time-honored phrase, "Violence is the last resort of the powerless."

People tend to resort to terrorism when they feel disenfranchised, that their group is being oppressed, and that the only chance they have of having their voices heard, and possibly achieving change, is to act out in violence. They are simultaneously striking a blow of revenge, while trying to draw attention to their plight – or perceived plight.

There are not freedom fighters. They are not insurgents. Freedom fighters and insurgents traditionally choose targets of the government that they hate, or choose targets that support the government that they hate. They do not want the people to fear them, as terrorists do. Instead, they want to break the stranglehold of power that the government, or repressive regime, has. They choose military targets. They choose government buildings. They choose people who work for the government.

Conversely, terrorists do not want to tackle the government that they hate in a direct fashion. They know that in a direct matchup with the government that they oppose, they will lose. Their primary goal in acts of terrorism is to strike at the people who empower the government which they, the terrorists, hate. Yes, revenge on a populace which has financed the actions of the government they hate may be a motivating factor in what they do. However the primary goal of terrorism is to convince "the enemy" that they themselves do not wish to engage in a long and bloodied struggle.

The mechanics are like this:

1. A group of people have a basic fundamental right which they feel is not being respected.
2. They feel that this fundamental right is being violated by a specific group of people or entity. (Usually a government or members of another religion.)
3. They feel that they have no hope of achieving this right through negotiations or some other normal political activity.
4. They also have no hope of achieving this right through direct military engagement.
5. They decide to attack the resolve of the oppressing group through asymmetrical attacks on the general population of the oppressing group.
6. This is done in the hope that a majority of the oppressing group, or its government, grows tired of bloodshed, and the fear of bloodshed, and decides the burdens of supporting the repressive actions outweigh the benefits of continuing with the repressive policies.

Usually, terrorist actions are met with hostility by the dominant group who then come up with new measures to "deal with the problem". These measures are usually an increase in security directives, which make the repressed group feel even more disenfranchised – which unfortunately leads to more people feeling that violence and terrorism is the only hope of ever having their rights respected.

At this point I want to make it abundantly clear that I am not taking sides or trying to preach what is right or wrong in these kinds of political conflicts. I am simply describing the mechanics of what commonly happens so that people can understand why terrorism takes place.

The problem is that any group which feels that their basic human rights are being violated can spiral down into this mindset when they feel that there is no hope, other than violence, to escape their oppression. According to the FBI data 42% of terror attacks carried out in America were carried out by Latinos. It is difficult to envision that Latinos in America feel that their religious rights are not being respected.

Maybe these terror attacks were related to dismay over America's immigration policies. Or maybe the FBI was labeling certain gang-related activities as terrorist acts.

Regardless, what the FBI statistics illustrate quite clearly is that no single ethnic group, political ideology, religion, or any other qualifier you could think up, has a monopoly on terrorism in America.

Terrorists come from all walks of life.

Some of them will shoot up Jewish synagogues over religion[17]; some will shoot up black churches over race hate[18]. Some will blow up a school because their mortgage is in arrears[19], some will shoot up a school because they are tired of being bullied[20]. Some will shoot up an Army base because they feel the government is waging war on their Islamic religion[21], while others will poison medical supplies for unknown reasons[22].

Airplanes into buildings, car bombs, machetes, sniping along the freeway, civil rights activists buried in swamps, anthrax in envelopes, blowing up embassies, suitcase bombs in lockers and airports, lynchings, "human hunting" at a McDonald's, and carefully handcrafted mail bombs…

The list seems endless.

But the common theme that runs among all of these attacks is that the people perpetrating them wanted attention. They felt repressed, they felt angry, and they wanted the recognition – and possible changes – that they foresaw their actions would bring.

They wanted the world to know what they had done. They wanted to leave their indelible mark in the collective psyche of American memory. They choose actions which were designed to make people far and wide afraid. The more death they could cause, the better. The softer and more sympathetic the target, the better.

There arises a certain trade-off that takes place when terrorists choose targets; some will opt for the most sympathetic targets so as to shock the conscience of the public. This group will opt for the most helpless targets possible, and take great relish in killing children, and otherwise causing as many collateral deaths as possible.

Some terrorists, however, decide that they can achieve maximum name recognition by striking a target that is as powerful as possible. The rationale behind this thinking is akin to, "If we can attack these people in the US Army base, what chance do you have of being safe whether you are going out to a shopping mall, or cowering under your bed at home?"

Thus, while the targets themselves may seem radically different, an elementary school as opposed to a US Army military installation here in the United States, the objective of both are the same. Both attacks are designed to make everyone in America afraid as they realize that they are never safe no matter where they are.

And more importantly, no one's family members, or other loved ones, are ever safe.

It is hoped by the terrorist that if that message is hammered home hard enough, the people will rise up and put enough pressure on their government to end the overall conflict which the terrorist feels is oppressing them.

Given this mindset of terrorists – their desire to be as sensationalistic as possible, while striking back at the government which is oppressing them, it is a certainty that Trump properties, and the people who visit them, work in them, or live in them – how long is it before the first Trump property is the target of a terror attack?

"[Terrorism has] gotten to a point where it's not even being reported, and in many cases the very, very dishonest press doesn't want to report it. They have their reasons and you understand that."

Donald J. Trump, Feb. 6, 2017

13 Trump's Obligation to Release Tenants from Their Leases.

The law is very clear — a landlord has a duty to mitigate and nullify any and all foreseeable hazards on their properties which threaten the safety of their guests, invitees, and tenants. Should a landlord fail in their duty to prevent these hazards which are foreseeable, the landlord is financially and otherwise civilly responsible — and sometimes criminally responsible — for the foreseeable harms which result from the breach of their duty.

If a landlord does not de-ice the walkways of an apartment complex within a reasonable period of time after the ice forms, they are responsible for the harm of somebody slipping and falling. This is basic law. It is so basic that all of you reading this who have never attended law school already knew it.

And Donald Trump has been sued by people for so many different things that it is impossible to believe that he does not know this.

How on earth could Donald Trump ever argue that he did not foresee terrorist attacks on his properties?

No, let me correct that question. How on earth could Donald Trump ever honestly argue that he did not foresee terrorist attacks on his properties?

Based upon the fact that America already employs great security to prevent attacks at the properties he normally visits, and the fact that the Secret Service has undoubtedly briefed him that he is more a terror target in his "Trump Tower" than at the White House, we know Donald Trump already knows that his properties are a prime target for terrorism.

We also know that were he to place his properties in a blind trust, no one would know which properties he still owned and which ones he would not own. Only the trustee would know. Donald Trump would not know. ISIS would not know. Al Qaeda would not know. Far-left liberals who were edging towards violence would not know. The surviving Branch Davidians would not know.

In short, no terrorists or budding terrorists would know.

But Donald Trump refuses to take this step. He refuses to place his properties into a blind trust. Previously I stated the man's wallet was surpassed only by his ego, but I now realize that is an incorrect statement – larger than the man's wallet or his ego is his cavalier disregard for human life other than his own.

If Donald Trump had a smidgen of conscience in that brain of his he would place his properties into a blind trust, or at the very least offer to allow his tenants to break their leases with him if they so chose. He would inform them of the potential risk of terrorism at his properties, as it is a known and foreseeable risk that he has already been briefed on, and allow the tenants to decide if they want to stay or leave. It would be the very least that a man with any shred of conscience would do.

But we all know Donald Trump is not going to offer them the opportunity to be released from their leases. We know this because when Trump took over a golf course in Jupiter Florida he changed the name to Trump National Golf Club, and changed many of the terms and conditions of membership. Many of the members exercised their legal option to leave, and Donald Trump made sure each and every one of them got stiffed on their refund fees. That is correct—when Trump took over the golf club, and unilaterally changed the terms and conditions of membership, over 150 members decided to leave. So what did Donald Trump do? He ordered that ALL of their deposits be kept, and they continue to be billed for membership.

Donald Trump takes it as a great insult when anybody bristles at his exercise of unilateral and dictatorial powers. He wants HIS money!

Ultimately, the court forced the club to refund $5.7 million that it had effectively stolen from its members when they decided to leave Trump's club.

So we know Trump does not like to let people out of their contractual obligations, even when he is the one who has changed the terms and conditions. That means Donald Trump is not going to allow anybody in any of these properties I have listed, or others he owns that I have not listed which are also available through a basic level Google search, out of their lease. His position will be that each and every one of these properties is more valuable now that he is President and that the increase in value is easily worth all of the possible deaths that occur.

What that ultimately means is when those terror attacks take place, no matter what form they are, the victims of those attacks will be forced to drag Donald Trump into court to seek redress for his action of inviting terrorism onto his properties, and not placing said properties into a blind trust as other Presidents have done.

Trump will publicly decry the legal actions, of course. He will scream they are without merit. He will invent shadow enemies that are financing the spurious attacks. He will dredge up the ethnic group or gender of the judge(s) and plaintiffs to attack them.

But, as Trump almost always does in legal proceedings, he will settle, or lose.

"SEE YOU IN COURT, THE SECURITY OF OUR NATION IS AT STAKE!"

Donald J. Trump, Feb. 9, 2017

14 A Call for Legislation... Or Constitutional Amendment... Or... At Least the Courts...

Even as I write this, word is out that the Saudis have been leasing space from Donald Trump in his Trump International Hotel on Pennsylvania Avenue. How nice of the same people that gave us ALL nineteen 9-11 Hijackers – but conveniently did NOT make Donald Trump's 7-country banned list – have been piping money to him by leasing property space from him.

Hey, like I said, if the American people are willing to tolerate such obvious corruption in the President, who am I to argue? When Americans decide to address the issue of Trump's corruption using whatever legitimate means gets the job done, they will do so.

But, let's look beyond arguing which foreign power—the House of Saud or the iron fist of Putin – owns Trump more[23]. What we need to look at is the fact that each and every Trump property—especially those that bear his name—are subject to terrorist attacks. They are obvious and inviting targets that beg the major terrorist powers and the deluded loners to make their play for glory.

It doesn't have to be ISIS that goes for the bragging rights of having attacked a handful of tenants in a Trump property—remember, Columbine was just 2 teenagers with some guns and way too much ammo.

That is all it takes.

We need laws that require a President to place assets that other people rent and use into a blind trust so that these soft targets are gone. We need Congress to pass these laws.

And, we need them now.

Yes, I know, I know, I know. The Constitution might not allow Congress to require such an action. There is a Separation of Powers Doctrine, and what would the penalty be if the President refused? Congress nullify the vote of the People and that person is no longer President?

Yeah, I doubt it would get past the Supreme Court. Unless the Constitution is modified requiring...

Yeah, I can't finish the sentence. It isn't going to happen. Nothing feasible and prudent can force a President to place his assets into a blind trust while he, or she, is President. If the People are willing to tolerate such an open invitation to outside influence, so be it. Let Donald Trump funnel his bribes openly through his various commercial ventures with the favors purchased publicly handed out by Trump.

But the first time a terrorist harms or kills someone on one of his properties that he did not place into a blind trust, let the President be liable to each and every victim for every penny of harm. The Courts cannot force good behavior, but they have a long history of punishing bad behavior. The attacks on Trump properties are not merely foreseeable, but rather it will be a miracle if we go through his (hopefully short) presidency without a few major attacks on his properties. That means Trump, himself, should foot the bill out of his own pocket when terrorists attack one of his commercial ventures.

And, Donald Trump does not get Presidential/Governmental immunity! He, Donald Trump, the greedy lucre-loving business mogul has decided to pursue a course of action in his business dealings which subject his customers to a much heightened risk of personal harm, and/or death.

That is NOT Donald Trump acting as President. That is Donald Trump acting as a greedy, soulless, POS robber baron. He has the right to keep his commercial ventures separate from the Office of President, but that also means he does not receive Executive immunity for his decisions which he, Donald Trump filthy rich businessman, makes as the owner of private property.

That means that when the terrorists start taking down all those soft targets he has, because it was a foreseeable risk that he, greedy, soulless POS robber baron Donald Trump chose in his private capacity to ignore, he should be personally liable for each and every penny of loss.

Out of his own pocket.

Let's see how many terror attacks and lives Donald Trump is willing to risk when it is his coin compensating the victims of his corrupt decisions and greed....

Endnotes

[1] I do acknowledge there is some debate over whether or not we shot it down, including Donald Rumsfeld having referred to it, perhaps in a Freudian Slip, as having been "shot down". Dick Cheney, in another interview calmly referred in detail to having given the order to shoot it down. However, there is debate as to whether or not the order was actually carried out before the passengers brought down the plane themselves.

[2] Harwell, Brittain, O'Connell, "Trump family's elaborate lifestyle is a 'logistical nightmare' — at taxpayer expense", the Washington Post, Feb. 16, 2017, https://www.washingtonpost.com/business/economy/trump-familys-elaborate-lifestyle-a-logistical-nightmare--at-taxpayer-expense/2017/02/16/763cce8e-f2ce-11e6-a9b0-ecee7ce475fc_story.html

[3] From "Gimme What You Got" by Don Henley, 1989, off the "End Of The Innocence" album/CD.

[4] I am assuming the people that would attend the Mar-a-Lago Country Club would use either ketchup or cracked crab. Both of these might be too cheap for people of such wealth to ever consume, but I will never know.

[5] He owns several, of course.

[6] The fact that Donald Trump has publicly stated on the Howard Stern show that he likes to walk into the dressing rooms of these underage girls unannounced, and while they are undressed, would only make it more personal an attack. Now they get to target what they view as his "concubines". In short, attacking a Miss Teen USA pageant is attacking Donald Trump right in the crotch.

[7] Doubtful—some estimates place him at less than half that amount, while

others place it down to under $1B.

[8] Please do not assume I am being creative here. This is such a known real threat that the US Postal Service began installing anthrax detectors in their main processing centers back in 2003.

[9] Sherman, Erik. "A Look Inside Donald Trump's Lavish, $200 Million 'Palace'". Fortune. Retrieved November 18, 2016.

[10] http://washington.dc.retailguide.com/data/m100523.htm

[11] https://property.compstak.com/40-Wall-Street-New-York/p/1375

[12] http://www.teenvogue.com/story/donald-trump-colognes-discontinued-reason

[13] https://www.bloomberg.com/politics/articles/2016-03-09/when-trump-steaks-at-a-trump-event-aren-t-really-trump-steaks

[14] https://property.compstak.com/725-5th-Avenue-New-York/p/587

[15] https://www.documentcloud.org/documents/2175187-trump.html

[16] See: Center for Research on Globalization, Non-Muslims Carried Out More than 90% of All Terrorist Attacks in America, January 28, 2017, Global Research, at http://www.globalresearch.ca/non-muslims-carried-out-more-than-90-of-all-terrorist-attacks-in-america/5333619

[17] Overland Park Jewish Community Center shooting, April 13, 2014

[18] Charleston church shooting, Charleston church shooting

[19] Bath School Disaster, May 18, 1927

[20] Columbine shooting, April 20, 1999

[21] Fort Hood shooting, November 5, 2009

[22] Chicago Tylenol murders, September, 1982.

[23] Besides, we already know it is Putin.

About the Author

K.D. Bellston is a retired business owner who has settled into a life of writing, normally in the area of socially conscious human resources management. When asked why the foray into a political endeavor such as this book, Bellston responded:

"I started life as a conservative, being enraptured by Reagan's stated philosophies of small government and self-reliance. Over time, I have watched that conservative ideology turn into a vicious beast that has fixated upon two primary goals: 1.) Turning America into a Christian theocracy, and 2.) Using whatever governmental power and violence are necessary to maximize the profits of the rich and superrich. This has led us to the insanity where Christian Fundamentalists are joyously embracing the teachings of a man who openly brags about the fact he likes to, "Grab married women by the pussy", and the fact that he could kill somebody in public and his followers would still blindly adhere to him.

Since this is the new face of "conservatism" in America, I want nothing to do with it. The fascists[24] have taken over and I will neither help them, nor stand by idly. Instead, I want to try and help expose the new conservatism for the evil and virulent authoritarianism and fascism that it is.

The Founding Fathers believed in individual freedom to live one's life unfettered by religious and governmental mandates, and that government existed to protect the Nation from external threats and promote individual liberty. That is what I believed back then, and still believe. Trump and his ilk... I just can't remain silent while he and his followers try to seize power by gutting the Constitution and trampling on the Rights of the People."

K.D. Bellston can be reached at:

Facebook: www.facebook.com/K.D.Bellston
Twitter: @K_D_Bellston
LinkedIn: K.D. Bellston
Tumblr: k-d-bellston.tumblr.com

---

[24] From Wikipedia:

"Fascists believe that liberal democracy is obsolete, and they regard the complete mobilization of society under a totalitarian one-party state as necessary to prepare a nation for armed conflict and to respond effectively to economic difficulties. Such a state is led by a strong leader—such as a dictator and a martial government composed of the members of the governing fascist party—to forge national unity and maintain a stable and orderly society. Fascism rejects assertions that violence is automatically negative in nature, and views political violence, war, and imperialism as means that can achieve national rejuvenation. Fascists advocate a mixed economy, with the principal goal of achieving autarky through protectionist and interventionist economic policies."

www.ingramcontent.com/pod-product-compliance
Lightning Source LLC
Chambersburg PA
CBHW072213280526
45788CB00002B/1005